Ludwig van Beethoven

The Life, Times, & Music™ Series

Ludwig van Beethoven

The Life, Times, & Music™ Series

Judith Mahoney Pasternak

FRIEDMAN/FAIRFAX

PUBLISHERS

ACKNOWLEDGMENTS

Thanks to Chris Seymour and Ellen Davidson for reading parts
of this manuscript, to my editor, Hallie Einhorn, for her skill,
and to the Friedman Group's Nathaniel Marunas, for his guidance
in the early stages of this book. And thanks, most of all,
to my parents: Bill Mahoney, who taught me writing,
and Bea Kelvin, who taught me Beethoven.

A FRIEDMAN/FAIRFAX BOOK

ISBN 1-56799-184-X

Editor: Hallie Einhorn
Art Director: Jeff Batzli
Designer: Andrea Karman
Photography Editor: Jennifer Crowe McMichael
Production Manager: Jeanne Kaufman

Grateful acknowledgment is given to authors, publishers, and photographers for permission to
reprint material. Every effort has been made to determine copyright owners of photographs and
illustrations. In the case of any omissions, the publishers will be pleased to make suitable
acknowledgments in future editions.

Printed in the United States of America by Quebecor Printing Semline, Inc.

For bulk purchases and special sales, please contact:
Friedman/Fairfax Publishers
Attention: Sales Department
15 West 26th Street
New York, New York 10010
(212) 685-6610 FAX (212) 685-1307

Contents

Introduction 6

Bonn, 1770 10

No Time for Childhood (1770–1782) 16

A Very Young Composer (1782–1791) 22

To Vienna (1792–1794) 30

A Legend in Embryo (1795–1802) 38

Crisis After Crisis (1802–1812) 46

The Woman He Loved 56

Everything but Joy (1812–1824) 59

Finale (1825–1827) 66

Suggested Reading 69

Suggested Listening 69

Index 71

Introduction

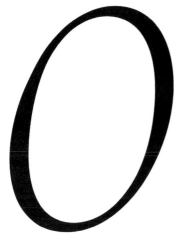

ld Europe was giving birth to its modern self in the eighteenth century. Turbulence was the order of the day in every facet and dimension of life, from the economic, political, and social to the technological and cultural.

New wealth was pouring into Europe; new forms of wealth were being created; and new segments of society were acquiring large parts of that wealth. The old aristocracies were reluctantly giving way economically

This painting, which depicts the wedding celebration of Emperor Joseph II in 1760, captures the glittering extravagance of the old aristocracy.

to the rising merchants—and, later,

industrialists—situated in the so-

cial hierarchy between the nobility

and peasantry. The prosperity of

The defining moment of eighteenth-century Europe: the capture of the Bastille, July 14, 1789.

these new "middle" classes in turn

fueled the fight for political power, a

struggle that shaped and was shaped

by revolutionary democratic visions

of liberty, equality, and fraternity.

The new forces also made their

mark on high culture, until then the

preserve of the nobility. In its newly

broadened and accessible forms as

well as in its contents, the culture re-

flected the turmoil of the times and

the lives and concerns of the people

creating it.

Ludwig van Beethoven, whose music captured the sweeping changes of his time, led the way for all nineteenth-century composers.

In such a climate, anything could happen. Genius could rise from any corner and find its own level. The son of a Corsican lawyer could become an emperor and change the boundaries of Europe; the son of an obscure German court tenor could become one of the greatest composers of all time and change the nature of music forever.

Bonn, 1770

If the old order was passing, the ancient city of Bonn, located on the Rhine, had not yet heard the news.

Paris and Vienna might have been in ferment, but Bonn was only a western fragment of the overextended, moribund Holy Roman Empire. It was the seat, as it had been since 1257, of the Archbishop-Elector of Cologne, its academy still fourteen years

The city of Bonn, Beethoven's birthplace.

away from obtaining university status.

Yet the arts flourished in eighteenth-century Bonn in the court of Elector Maximilian Friedrich. The ideas of the Enlightenment that were turning Europe upside down —including the politics of liberalization (if not yet democratization) and

The elder Ludwig van Beethoven, the composer's grandfather.

the artistic seeds of what would become romanticism—were alive and under much discussion at the academy.

The arts had nowhere but the court in which to flourish. There were, as yet, few independent artists marketing their creations to paying audiences. Some artists would begin to do so over the next half-century, in part because of the determination and courage of a man born in Bonn in December 1770 who was destined to become the old town's most famous son. At the time, however, an artistic or musical career still depended on the patronage of a court, where artists and musicians enjoyed relatively high job security and the relatively low status of upper servants. Two generations of the Beethoven family were in service as musicians to Elector Maximilian Friedrich: Ludwig van Beethoven (1712–1773), grandfather to the world-renowned composer bearing the same name, served as Kapellmeister, or director of the court orchestra; and his son Johann (c. 1739–1792) served as court tenor.

Currents of Change: Europe, 1770–1827

Opposites clashed; contradiction flourished; paradox compounded paradox. Gold stolen from the peoples of Asia, Africa, and the Americas lined the pockets of Europe's old nobility and of its new middle classes as well, who responded with the idea that all men are created equal.

That was the Europe into which Beethoven was born in 1770. During his lifetime—he died in 1827—Beethoven would see the beginning of both the Industrial Revolution and the population explosion (Europe had 120 million inhabitants in 1700, 180 million in 1800); the French Revolution; a continent-wide wave of counterrevolution and repression; and various radical reconfigurations of the map of Europe. He would himself be a major figure in an equally profound transformation of the content, production, and consumption of European culture.

The state was being tossed by opposing currents from every direction, becoming at once broader-based and more centralized. Under feudalism, monarchs had been merely firsts among equals—rulers not over states, but over aristocracies that in turn ruled their own lands all but absolutely. However, in the century preceding Beethoven's birth, the new middle classes demanded a greater share of participation in government.

In the mid-eighteenth century, three monarchs embraced parts of the rationalist, humanitarian trend collectively called the Enlightenment. Frederick the Great (1712–1786) of Prussia, Maria Theresa (1717–1780) of Austria, and Catherine the Great (1729–1796) of Russia all liberalized their countries to some degree. (Maria Theresa's son and co-ruler, Joseph II [1741–1790], went so far as to free Austria's serfs.) Yet these monarchs also centralized and strengthened their kingdoms, creating administrative bureaucracies that provided work for the outmoded nobilities.

These rulers were also territorially ambitious. Along with Beethoven's sometime-hero, Napoleon Bonaparte (1769–1821), as well as with Napoleon's enemies, they made and remade the map of Europe repeatedly during Beethoven's lifetime. War was virtually continuous. The old great powers were fading; Austria, Russia, and Prussia grew at the expense of the Holy Roman Empire, the Ottoman Empire, and Poland.

The move toward democracy culminated first with the American Revolution of 1776, then with the French Revolution that began in 1789. During Beethoven's lifetime, France was the source of the single greatest storm to buffet Europe. First the Revolution created a republic, preached liberty, equality, and fraternity, and guillotined its monarchs, Louis XVI (1754–1793) and his wife Marie Antoinette (1755–1793); Europe's collective royalty quaked for their heads and crowns. Then the upstart Bonaparte created an empire, causing them to fear for their territories. Napoleon's defeat in 1815 triggered widespread repression, but it was too late; democratization was inevitable. The turmoil would last, with brief respites, through the revolutions of 1848 and the more radical analyses of socialism and communism to the end of the century and beyond.

The philosophers and writers of the Enlightenment—the satirist François Marie Arouet de Voltaire (1694–1778), the encyclopedist Denis Diderot (1713–1784), and the philosopher Jean-Jacques Rousseau (1712–1778) in France; the Scottish liberal philosopher David Hume (1711–1776); and the German philosopher Immanuel Kant (1724–1804)—had among them provided the intellectual underpinnings of democratization. The German philosopher Georg Wilhelm Friedrich Hegel (1770–1831) went further; history, he said, progressed dialectically; movement in any direction engendered

Indelibly etched in the French collective consciousness: Delacroix's Liberty Leading the People.

its opposite until synthesis resolved each clash. It was a theory for the times; it was also essentially conservative, implying that whatever is, is right for the moment. Ironically, Karl Marx (1818–1883) half a century later would make Hegel's dialectic the foundation of his revolutionary theories.

The arts were in ferment as well. Formerly protégés of the aristocracy, artists now increasingly lived like everyone else, selling their wares in the marketplace. Beethoven's father and grandfather both spent their careers as glorified servants in the court of the Elector of Cologne; in contrast, Beethoven, though he still received substantial assistance from individual counts and princes, made much of his living by performing in public concerts and publishing his music.

Not coincidentally, the content of artistic output was also transformed. The formal, ordered, balanced—in a word, aristocratic—ideal of classical art gave way to the impassioned, liberty-loving and individualistic ideal of romanticism.

In literature, the English romantics— William Blake (1757–1827), William Wordsworth (1770–1850), Samuel Taylor Coleridge (1772–1834), George Gordon, Lord Byron (1788–1824), Percy Bysshe Shelley (1792–1822), and John Keats (1795–1821)—and the German writers Johann von Goethe (1749–1832) and Friedrich Schiller (1759–1805) gave voice to the new spirit.

Visual artists across Europe freed themselves from the formal constraints of baroque art as they depicted the new freedoms. French painters, especially Jacques Louis David (1748–1825) and Eugène Delacroix (1798–1863) celebrated revolution; a little later, the Spanish painter Francisco de Goya (1746–1828) graphically protested Napoleon's savage onslaught in Spain. In England, Blake's mystical, fantastic paintings and engravings broke new stylistic ground, and the landscapes of Joseph Turner (1775–1851) prefigured the impressionism that would arise later in the century.

But in the world of music, one man alone formed the bridge between the classicism of Mozart and Haydn and the romanticism that followed. Out of that entire revolutionary period, it would be Beethoven's name that reverberated through history as *the* revolutionary of music. It would also be his life that reverberated as the life of the romantic artist.

Born to a baker in Malines, near Antwerp, in an area that was ceded to Austria as the Austrian Netherlands a year after his birth, the elder Ludwig van Beethoven was trained as a musician in his hometown. In 1733, when he was twenty-one years old, Ludwig came to Bonn, where he almost immediately found employment in the court as well as a wife, Maria Josefa Pols (1714–1775). Only nineteen years old at the time, the bride presumably showed no sign of the penchant for drink that would later afflict both herself and her son Johann.

Of Ludwig and Maria Josefa's three children, only Johann survived infancy. He was trained in his father's trade. As a child he sang in the court choir, which he was officially entered into in 1756. Sometime during the next few years, Maria Josefa's drinking became of such concern that she was sent away to a nunnery. (The family was nominally Roman Catholic, but there is little evidence that any of them were particularly devout.)

Maria Josefa never returned home, leaving Ludwig and Johann on their own. Father and son lived together until 1767, when Johann, then in his late twenties, traveled up the Rhine to nearby Ehrenbreitstein in search of a bride. He returned with the young widow Maria Magdalena Leym (1746–1787), née Keverich,

Beethoven's father, Johann van Beethoven.

14

daughter of the chief kitchen
overseer of a noble's palace
in Ehrenbreitstein. Ludwig
described the young woman
as a "maid" and objected to
her vehemently, but Johann
married her anyway; it was
one of the few times in his
life that Johann ever overtly
defied his father. Ludwig
moved to a nearby lodging,
and Johann and Maria
Magdalena began what was
to be their tumultuous life
together. (By all accounts,
it was Johann, and never
Maria Magdalena, who
was the instigator of the
turbulence.) The couple's
first child was born and

Beethoven's mother, Maria Magdalena.

baptized Ludwig Maria in the spring of 1769, but unfortunately
the infant survived for only a few days.

A year and a half later, Maria Magdalena gave birth to their
second child. Apparently determined to give Johann's father a
namesake, the proud parents christened the new baby Ludwig, too,
but this time left out the middle name Maria. Although the exact
date of birth is unknown, it was almost certainly only a day or two
before the child was baptized as Ludwig van Beethoven on
December 17, 1770.

No Time for Childhood (1770–1782)

The Beethovens were not a happy family, nor was little Ludwig a happy child.

He had little reason to be happy. His father, Johann, was a drunkard, a bully, and a mediocrity who commanded little respect in his own family, which was still ruled over by the elder Ludwig.

The house where Beethoven lived in Bonn.

One of Beethoven's pianos.

The grandfather may well have stood between his only grandchild and the worst of Johann's tempers; Maria Magdalena apparently could not. As an adult, Beethoven was vociferous on almost every subject except that of his childhood; when he did talk about this part of his life, he spoke of his mother with love, the elder Ludwig with reverence, and his father not at all.

But Beethoven's grandfather died a week or so after his third birthday. (His grandmother, Maria Josefa, died two years later, but she had lived away from the family for so long that her passing had little impact on anyone except, perhaps, the son who so tragically took after her.) Maria Magdalena was pregnant at the time of her father-in-law's death, and in April of the following year, she gave birth to Caspar Carl van Beethoven (1774–1815).

It was around this time that Johann decided to use little Ludwig to reach for the success that had eluded him. With the young Wolfgang Amadeus Mozart (1756–1791) nearing adulthood, there might be room in Europe for a new wunderkind, and Johann tried hard to train Ludwig for the role. By the time Beethoven was four, he was practicing the piano—by all reports, less than enthusiastically—for several hours a day. The sessions were strict and joyless. Johann hated the boy's attempts to improvise and badgered him constantly to play only the notes set down on the

An advertisement for Beethoven's first public performance.

page before him. A neighbor later declared that the young Beethoven often cried while he played. It was not long after instituting piano lessons that Johann added violin to the curriculum.

Maria Magdalena bore another son, Nikolaus Johann (1776–1846), shortly before Ludwig's sixth birthday. The family sent Ludwig to school, but without Johann to bully him into performing, he was a less-than-stellar pupil. Dreamy and surly, often unkempt and dirty, the boy learned little and made few friends.

No one cared, except perhaps the lonely child. He was making progress as a musician, but he was not yet (and indeed never would be) the child prodigy Johann desired; Johann himself may have impeded the early development of his genius son with the ban on improvisation. Nevertheless, Ludwig was ready for his first concert before he was eight years old. On March 26, 1778, he appeared in Cologne, performing in a program of concertos and trios.

Little Ludwig's first professional piano teacher, Christian Gottlob Neefe.

In February 1779, Maria Magdalena bore her first daughter, Anna Maria, but the baby lived for only two days. Not long afterward, Johann brought home a drinking companion, Tobias Pfeifer, to teach eight-year-old Ludwig how to play the piano. Little is known about Pfeifer except that he and Johann would wake Ludwig for lessons when they came roistering home from the taverns.

In November of the same year, however, Christian Gottlob Neefe (1748–1798), a composer and musician of some note, arrived in Bonn. Johann immediately hired him to replace Pfeifer. The new instructor and his pupil formed a close relationship that was to endure for the rest of Neefe's life. Years after the lessons with Neefe had ended, Beethoven wrote to his former instructor, "Should I ever become a great man, you too will have had a share in my success."

Ferdinand Ries, one of Beethoven's early biographers.

It was probably around the same time that Ludwig began taking violin lessons with Franz Ries (1755–1846), whose son Ferdinand (1784–1838) would become Beethoven's friend and eventually one of his biographers. Beethoven would have many other teachers (including Europe's foremost composer, Joseph Haydn, as well as Nikolaus Simrock [1751–1832], the future music publisher). Over the next twenty years, he studied piano, organ, violin, horn, and various aspects of composition. Often, a relatively brief teacher-pupil relationship would be followed by a more prolonged but unstable friendship.

In January 1781, Maria Magdalena bore yet another son, Franz Georg. She had little time, and Johann little interest, in Ludwig's academic career, a career that was coming to an inglorious end. Later that year, Ludwig dropped out of school.

In November, Ludwig went with Maria Magdalena on the first long trip of his life—a voyage down the Rhine to Rotterdam. He must have felt very grown-up, accompanying his mother (and, presumably, infant brother) on the boat. He was no longer attending school like the other children; his life at home consisted of music, music, and more music.

In 1782, Neefe arranged for a firm in Mannheim to publish Ludwig's set of nine piano variations on a march by Ernst Christoph Dressler. (Beethoven's first published work, these variations are now known as WoO 63.) Ludwig's childhood, such as it had been, was over. He was eleven years old.

Nikolaus Simrock taught music to Beethoven briefly, then became one of his most important publishers.

A Very Young Composer (1782–1791)

An eleven-year-old who was finished with school was virtually an adult in the eighteenth century; there was no concept of adolescence as we now know it. Beethoven entered young adulthood composing steadily, all the while earning more than his keep at court.

It is worth noting the way in which Beethoven's compositions are numbered. Beethoven himself assigned the opus numbers to virtually all his major works, although a few were given, for better or worse, by music publishers. However, there were hundreds of pieces that Beethoven considered to be too insubstantial to merit an opus number. In the 1950s, musicologists Georg Kinsky and Willy Hess separately cataloged all the extant, previously unnumbered works, which have been known since by either a Hess number or a WoO ("Work without Opus number") given by Kinsky.

Beethoven did not give opus numbers to any of the compositions he wrote during his youth and adolescence in Bonn. Many, especially the earliest surviving pieces, are indeed slight, consisting primarily of piano works—sonatas, rondos, and variations—as well as songs. His music was rooted in the late classical style of Mozart and Haydn; the early Bonn chamber works, written from the time he was eighteen or nineteen, were lighthearted pieces designed to entertain the elector and his court.

For it was through the court and the elector—Maximilian Friedrich until 1784, and then Maximilian Franz (1756–1801), brother of Emperor Joseph II—that Beethoven was making a living, thanks to his own talents and the help of his teacher. At first, the best that Neefe could do for the young composer was to have him appointed as unpaid assistant court organist in 1782 (it was more than Johann had been able to accomplish). But in a notice

A formal portrait by Joseph Engelbert Marteleux of Beethoven's first employer, Maximilian Friedrich, Archbishop and Elector of Cologne.

in the March 2, 1783, edition of Cramer's *Magazin der Musik*, Neefe glowingly described his young pupil as "a boy of eleven years old" (Beethoven was already twelve, but the article may have been written the previous year) who was "of most promising talent." Shortly afterward, the court orchestra hired the youth as a salaried cembalist (the word means harpsichordist, but the orchestra's cembalist was, in fact, a kind of assistant conductor).

Stephan von Breuning was the first of a series of young men with whom Beethoven maintained an ardent friendship.

It was an astonishing year for Ludwig. Still only twelve years old, he published a rondo (WoO 48), a song (WoO 107), and three sonatas (WoO 47). He also composed a fugue for the organ (WoO 31). Although life at home remained unhappy (his baby brother Franz Georg died that August), Ludwig had found a surrogate family, the first of a long series; the widow and children of a court official named von Breuning welcomed the young Beethoven into their home, first as a friend, and then as a piano teacher. Stephan von Breuning (1774–1827), became a lifelong friend, as did his sister Eleonore (1771–1841). Eleonore married Franz Gerhard Wegeler (1765–1848), who later collaborated with Ferdinand Ries on an early biography of Beethoven.

Beethoven's Music

Beethoven won his place in the musical pantheon not only through the grandeur of his work, but also through its profound influence on those who came after him. Almost single-handedly, he brought European composed music into the modern era. The last classical composer and the first romantic, Beethoven gave orchestral music the size, sweep, and passion of the nineteenth century and graced chamber music with a depth that his predecessors had never even imagined.

Beethoven did not begin as a musical revolutionary, but as a child writing Mozart-inspired musical diversions in the Bonn court. Mapping the path from the Variations on a March by Dressler to the Ninth Symphony and the final six string quartets, scholars have divided his output into an early, formative period; a middle, heroic period; and a final, transcendent period.

The first includes all of his youthful work from Bonn plus that of his first ten years in Vienna. Originally influenced by Mozart (and by his own teacher Christian Gottlob Neefe), Beethoven wrote primarily piano music and songs, enlarging his scope with the cantatas for two emperors after he came under Haydn's influence. Once in Vienna, Beethoven began to work out his own distinctive music; by 1802, he had written his first symphony, his first two piano concertos, and the "Pathétique" and "Moonlight" piano sonatas.

It was during his middle period, the extraordinary decade following 1802, that Beethoven composed much of his orchestral music. He was writing not for the chamber-size orchestra of Mozart's day, but for the larger orchestra of the modern concert hall; he was finding a musical vocabulary for the romantic spirit. During this time, Beethoven wrote the final version of his only opera, *Fidelio* (originally called "Leonora," the name still attached to its overture); Piano Concertos Nos. 3, 4, and 5 (the "Emperor"); his single violin concerto and the Triple Concerto for Piano, Cello, and Violin; and five symphonies. (The opening of the Fifth Symphony—the four-note "fate knocks at the door" motif—is probably the best-known musical phrase ever written.) Yet he also composed ever more daring chamber music; if the string quartets of Opus 18

Beethoven's sketches for Fidelio.

looked back to the classical period, the Razumovsky Quartets, with their innovative incorporation of Russian folk tunes, looked startlingly forward.

Then, in the last fifteen years of his life—the "transcendent" period—Beethoven went far beyond anything anyone, even he himself, had ever written. He redefined the symphony with his Seventh, Eighth, and Ninth ("Choral") Symphonies, then broke the last bastion of classicism with the final six string quartets. Passionate yet intellectual, longer than many Mozart and Haydn symphonies, these last quartets depart not only from the structural formalism of classical chamber music, but from its harmonic strictures as well. The unprecedented crashing and sustained dissonances of these works were Beethoven's ultimate contribution, pushing music into the nineteenth century—and beyond, into our own time.

During the 1780s, the teenage composer continued to study with Neefe, Ries, and others; to publish music; to teach; and to gain ever more important—and better-paying—positions at court. Changes in the court after the succession of the emperor's Enlightenment-influenced brother, Maximilian Franz, in 1784 had little impact on Beethoven's career. Ludwig was appointed court organist that same year.

In 1786, Beethoven's mother, then forty years of age, bore her last child, a daughter named Maria Margaretha. Like the last two, the baby did not survive long. The many childbirths and the strains of life with Johann were beginning to show on poor Maria Magdalena.

In the spring of 1787, Beethoven went to Vienna presumably to meet with—and perhaps even play for—Mozart. No one knows, however, whether the two most celebrated of Western composers ever actually met. In any case, Beethoven did not remain in Vienna for long; in July, he was recalled home by letters indicating that his mother was seriously ill.

"She was suffering from consumption," he wrote a few weeks later, "and in the end she died...after enduring great pain and agony. She was such a good, kind mother to me, and indeed, my best friend. Oh, who was happier than I when I could still utter the sweet name of mother...and to whom can I say it now?"

Back in Bonn, Beethoven kept composing despite his grief over his mother's death. It was also in 1787 that he wrote an early draft of what several years later he would rework as the Piano Concerto No. 2, Op. 19. That early draft is the first version we have of any of Beethoven's numbered opuses. The young composer was maturing.

Wolfgang Amadeus Mozart was the toast of Europe during his youth. When he reached adulthood, though, life became a constant struggle. Around the time that Beethoven first visited Vienna, Mozart was composing some of his greatest works— including Don Giovanni.

Later that year, Beethoven acquired his first patron, Count Ferdinand Waldstein (1762–1823), to whom he would later dedicate one of his finest piano sonatas, the Sonata No. 21 in C, Op. 53. By the next year, in addition to his work at court, Beethoven was playing regularly in the opera orchestra; he performed at least once in Mozart's *Die Entführung aus dem Serail* ("The Abduction from the Seraglio").

Emperor Leopold II, around the time of his 1790 accession. Still in Bonn at this time, Beethoven wrote a cantata for the occasion; later, he wanted Haydn to assure him that the cantata equaled Haydn's greatest works.

The years 1789 and 1790 brought major changes. Late in 1789, Johann retired from his position in court. Although barely fifty years old, he was ravaged by drink. The elector agreed to pay Johann's salary to Ludwig for the foreseeable future, though Ludwig, in order to save his father's pride, later arranged for the salary to be turned back over to Johann. Then, in 1790, the political climate of the Austrian Empire changed drastically with the death of the enlightened monarch Joseph II and the accession of his much more repressive brother, Leopold II. Still relatively uninterested in politics, Beethoven saw the twin events primarily as they affected his career; he wrote his two most ambitious works to date, a pair of cantatas on Joseph's death (WoO 87) and Leopold's accession (WoO 88).

Late the same year, the great Joseph Haydn, then Europe's most celebrated composer, came to Bonn. It is uncertain whether Haydn and Beethoven met on that visit, but they did spend time together when Haydn returned on his way back to Vienna a year and a half later. The meeting, a turning point in Beethoven's life, was to have a lasting impact on Haydn as well.

Joseph Haydn in his prime, about 1791. It was around that time that Haydn met Beethoven in Bonn and offered to take him on as a pupil.

To Vienna (1792–1794)

Haydn was sufficiently impressed with the young musician to propose that Beethoven come to Vienna and study with him.

Meanwhile, faraway events were striking the old town of Bonn with explosive force. In one of its first aggressive acts, the new French Republic occupied parts of the German Rhineland, causing the elector to flee in panic. The political turmoil and the tempting

Grillparzerhaus, one of Beethoven's many homes in Vienna.

Count Waldstein's prophetic farewell wishes to Beethoven, who was about to set off for the elegant city of Vienna.

invitation from the great Haydn—who, since Mozart's death the year before, had become Europe's preeminent living composer— persuaded Beethoven to set off for Vienna.

The invitation, however, raised the critical question of how Beethoven would make a living in the city. Although the sales of his compositions to publishers brought him some income, he was earning money in Bonn primarily by serving as a pianist in the elector's orchestra and by teaching.

Negotiations with the court secured the commitment to continue his salary through 1794. He would, of course, continue to compose and publish, and if he were lucky, he would acquire the patronage of the Viennese court or of an individual noble. The prospects were sufficiently promising, so in the fall of 1792, at age twenty-one, Beethoven prepared to leave the scene of his unhappy childhood. His early patron, Count Waldstein, thought highly enough of his talent as a composer to bid him farewell with the hope that he would "receive Mozart's spirit from Haydn's hands."

Joseph Haydn (1732–1809)

I t was a meeting of opposites when the tormented young composer and the old man whose very name represents the serene classical ideal first came face-to-face.

Haydn was sixty, apparently at the apex of his extraordinary career. Through his own efforts and the magnitude of his talent, this son of a wheelwright and a cook had crossed the still-rigid eighteenth-century class barriers to arrive at fame and intimacy with princes. Haydn obtained his early music education in a small church choir and then in the world-famous choir of Vienna's St. Stephen's Cathedral. When his voice broke, he was able to learn composition on his own and work his way up through the courts of the minor nobility. In 1760, he married Maria Anna Keller, and the following year he won a coveted assistant conductorship in the palace of the rich and influential Esterházy family of Eisenstadt, near Vienna. While the marriage was unhappy and unfruitful, the relationship with the Esterházys was a stunning success.

Haydn stayed with the family for thirty years, composing a lifetime's worth of music: cantatas and oratorios, over a dozen operas, 60 string quartets, 90 symphonies, and 126 trios for baryton (a now-obsolete stringed instrument that Prince Esterházy happened to play). The composer's renown increased as he mastered each form, synthesizing the formalism of the Baroque with the lighter style of the Austrian court and bringing the classical symphony to a peak of perfection. From 1782 on, he enjoyed a close friendship with Austria's other great genius, Wolfgang Amadeus Mozart, who was some twenty years his junior. When Haydn went to London in 1790, he had already lived out a success story marred only by marital discord (though he had found comfort in the company of a succession of other women).

Yet the best was still to come. London adored him, spurring him to new creative heights. During his year-and-a-half stay in this city, he received an honorary doctorate in music from Oxford University and composed some of his best-loved symphonies, including the "Surprise" Symphony, No. 94.

Mozart died while Haydn was in London, an event that may have left Haydn all the more open to the thought of nurturing young Ludwig van Beethoven's talents.

The relationship between Haydn and Beethoven turned out to be almost as tempestuous as Haydn's marriage, but nothing could block the aging composer's final creative outpouring. In his last fifteen years, Haydn wrote six more symphonies (including the beloved "Clock" Symphony, No. 101); five masses; a dozen great string quartets; hundreds of arrangements of British folk songs; the song "God Save the Emperor Francis" (which would later provide the melody for *Deutschland über alles*); and the two oratorios considered to be his masterpieces, *The Creation* and *The Seasons*.

Finally, though, age caught up with Haydn. He was ailing and bedridden when Napoleon's troops occupied Vienna in the spring of 1809; in a rare tribute, Napoleon ordered an honor guard to watch over Haydn's home. All Europe mourned when the great composer died on May 31, 1809.

Beethoven arrived in Vienna in November and almost immediately received word from Bonn of Johann's death. There is no record of how the composer took the news, no letter or diary entry like the emotional account he wrote after Maria Magdalena's death.

St. Stephen's Cathedral, in the heart of Vienna. Haydn sang in the choir here during his youth.

Still young, Beethoven was already irascible, eccentric, and temperamental. No matter what he did, though, Vienna came back for more.

His only extant comment is a letter written to the elector shortly thereafter requesting that monies that had been being paid to Johann now be paid over to him.

There is far more documentation of Beethoven's life in Vienna than of his childhood in Bonn. Like other literate people in that world without telephones, the composer wrote letters when he wanted to communicate with others. Thousands of these letters have been preserved. In addition, for two short periods in Vienna—including the two years immediately following his arrival there—Beethoven kept a sort of journal in which he recorded the mundane details of his daily life. Posterity knows more about how he settled into life in the big city than about how he composed his earliest works.

And settle in he did. Studying composition with Haydn, Beethoven also began to receive recognition as a pianist. In 1793, he was invited to move into the home of two of Vienna's important sponsors of music and musicians, Prince Karl (1761–1814) and Princess Christiane (1765–1841) Lichnowsky. The noble couple expected Beethoven to perform in their weekly musicales, yet their relationship with him grew to be more intimate than that of patrons with a mere protégé. They became another of his surrogate families; it was in their home that he wrote his Opus 1, three piano trios dedicated to the prince.

His compositions were still Mozartian and classical, but his piano playing was beginning to develop the style that would later be called romantic. An observer wrote, "[F]requently not an eye remained dry, while many would break out into loud sobs; for there was something wonderful in his expression, in addition to the beauty and originality of his ideas and his spirited style in rendering them."

Beethoven was also developing the idiosyncrasies that would haunt him forever. His lonely childhood—which would now be described as one of abuse—had left him ill-prepared for a career that

Beethoven playing the piano at a musicale held by the Prince and Princess Lichnowsky. Though the Lichnowskys never explicitly demanded Beethoven play for his supper, it was understood that he would oblige, at least from time to time.

involved tremendous amounts of socializing. He had little notion of how to interact appropriately with other people; he was needy and defensive with his friends, and rude, overbearing, and uncooperative with his generous patrons. He asked for more than people could give—even to the point of pressuring Haydn to concede that he, Beethoven, was already the old maestro's equal—and then interpreted their responses as insults or rejections. Perhaps most painfull of all, Beethoven never learned the most rudimentary forms of polite courtship.

Some part of the family weakness—alcoholism—may also have descended to Ludwig; certainly he consumed substantial quantities of wine, even for that heavy-drinking age. Perhaps not coincidentally, he expressed endless concern for his health, complaining often of respiratory and digestive problems. He filled page after page of letters and journals with wistful assertions that God and virtue alone sustained him.

In short, at age twenty-three, the composer was well on his way toward becoming the Beethoven of legend: tempestuous and irascible, touchy and demanding, careless of his appearance and slovenly in his habits, incapable of happiness, yet devoted to and exacting in his work. (Unlike Mozart, he was never facile; he corrected his compositions over and over, often reworking old pieces into new ones that pleased him more.) An increasingly romanticized Vienna soon perceived the temperamental Beethoven to be the very prototype of the artist. "Untamed," they called him; "an unlicked bear," someone said.

The first half of 1794 saw two events that would throw long shadows upon Beethoven's life: he stopped receiving his salary from Bonn, and his brother Caspar Carl came to Vienna.

A sketch of Beethoven's study in the Schwarzspanierhaus in Vienna.

A Legend in Embryo (1795–1802)

The loss of his salary from Bonn threw Beethoven on his own resources. Luckily, they were ample. For all the disasters that were to dog his footsteps during the rest of his life, Beethoven would never be hungry. Publishers clamored for the rights to put out his music. Music-intoxicated Viennese nobles vied with one another to help defray his living expenses. The Lichnowskys were ready to be second parents to him, despite the slight difference between his age and theirs; Prince Joseph Lobkowitz (1772–1816) and Count Andreas Razumovsky (1752–1836) offered patronage, too.

It was just as well. Beethoven needed several patrons so that when he quarreled with one or more—and quarrel he did, with more regularity than he did anything else except work—he had others to fall back on.

A still-youthful Beethoven conducting one of his chamber works in the salon of a Viennese noble.

However, it was not only with patrons that Beethoven argued. The irritable composer's anger was also set off by slights and injuries, real and imagined, as well as any oversolicitousness that he found to be patronizing or controlling. He rejected gifts as often as he accepted them, and by the middle of his first decade in Vienna he would no longer play the piano for his patrons. Perhaps he was unwilling to be at anyone's beck and call; perhaps he feared that his work would be plagiarized or his technique imitated. At least once, he claimed that a count or a prince had played one of his, Beethoven's, compositions without giving proper credit. The patrons forgave his refusal to play, as they forgave him for everything else.

Prince Joseph Lobkowitz, one of Beethoven's many patrons in Vienna.

Beethoven did play, however, for paying audiences. He was touring regularly, and in 1796 alone, he went on at least three trips, to Prague, Berlin, and Budapest. He gave concerts in Vienna as well, playing and conducting his own works as he churned them out.

And churn them out he would, with brief respites, for the rest of his life. The end of his so-called formative period had arrived. Beethoven was now writing familiar piano sonatas, trios, and

Johann Georg Albrechtsberger, composer and Kapellmeister in the court of Vienna. When Beethoven's appreciation of Haydn cooled, he turned to Albrechtsberger for lessons in composition.

concertos, like the 1799 Sonata in C Minor, Op. 13 (the "Pathetique") and the 1802 Sonata in C-sharp Minor, Op. 27/2 (the "Moonlight"). He also began to work in chamber and symphonic forms; in 1799, he conducted the first public performance of the Symphony No. 1 in C, Op. 21, and in 1801, he composed the six string quartets of Opus 18.

Not yet satisfied with his technical ability, Beethoven continued to study as well. When Haydn departed for a second trip to London in 1794, Beethoven seized the opportunity to take up a new teacher, the composer Johann Georg Albrechtsberger (1736–1809). Briefly in 1799, he studied with Antonio Salieri (1750–1825), best known to posterity for his rivalry with Mozart.

Antonio Salieri was an Italian-born composer who achieved success during his lifetime in the Viennese court but found everlasting fame as a rival of Mozart and a teacher of both Beethoven and Schubert.

In the heady atmosphere of sophisticated Vienna, Beethoven grew intellectually, too. The boy who had left school in Bonn at age ten with so few accomplishments had nevertheless learned to read a fair amount of French and some Latin and Italian, as well as his native German—and he never stopped reading. He had a lifelong habit of copying quotations that he found inspiring into letters and journals; his reading tastes for the most part matched those of his time. He often quoted the classics—Homer, Plato, and Plutarch, as well as Shakespeare—but he was also in touch with contemporary currents of thought. He particularly admired the poets Friedrich Schiller (1759–1805), whose "Ode to Joy" he would take as the text for one of the crowning achievements of his

An early Romantic vision of the poet: Goethe in the Country, *by Johann Tischbein.*

life, and Johann von Goethe (1749–1832), as well as the preeminent philosopher of the day, Immanuel Kant (1724–1804). ("The moral law within us and the starry sky above us—Kant!" Beethoven once wrote in a note, though when presented with the opportunity to hear Kant lecture in Vienna, he turned it down.)

Despite Beethoven's professional success and intellectual pursuits, his personal life was a shambles. His brothers had followed him to Vienna; Caspar Carl was working as a musician, and Nikolaus Johann, who had arrived in 1795, had obtained a job as a pharmacist's assistant. Beethoven perceived himself as the head of the reunited family and assumed the right, indeed the duty, to direct Caspar Carl and Nikolaus Johann in the most minute details of their lives. Their clashes were often loud and public. (Eventually, the composer would disapprove most heartily of both his brothers' marriages.)

Vienna, Austria, and the Habsburgs

A decade before Beethoven came to Vienna in 1792, Mozart had been welcomed to the glorious city with the assurance that "Here the fame of a man lasts only briefly."

It was that kind of town: glittering, pleasure-loving, cosmopolitan. It had been a city for three-quarters of a millennium, an imperial capital for three hundred years.

Founded on the Danube as Vindobona by the Romans at the end of the first century A.D., Vienna held a strategic position in central Europe. The Habsburgs, originally from Switzerland, had ruled the city since 1273; they had ruled Spain since 1516; and they had been Holy Roman Emperors since 1519. Their massive holdings had occasioned endless wars and power struggles across Europe. More than once at the losing end of a war, the Habsburgs had been forced to separate their Spanish and Holy Roman thrones, reuniting them the next time around.

Through it all, Vienna grew. Disasters thinned the population from time to time, but the city always attracted more people than it lost. One hundred thousand died from the plague in 1679, thousands more when the Turks laid siege in 1683. However, the Turks were defeated, and legend has it they left behind the coffee beans that gave rise to yet another of Vienna's wonderful attractions—its famous coffeehouses.

In 1740, Emperor Charles VI died without a male heir. He had willed most of the Habsburg possessions to his daughter, Maria Theresa, but no woman could succeed as Holy Roman Emperor. The ensuing War of the Austrian Succession (1740–1748) involved half of Europe, from Prussia to Spain; Maria Theresa's husband, Francis of Lorraine (1708–1765), was elected emperor of a shrunken Holy Roman Empire in 1745, but Habsburg Austria had expanded.

Their son, Joseph II, became Holy Roman Emperor and co-ruler of Austria, with Maria Theresa, in 1765. Though mother and son retained such prerogatives as the right to approve productions appearing in Viennese theaters, their reign was among the most liberal in Europe to that point. The accession in 1790 of Joseph's brother Leopold II ended liberalism with the implementation of censorship and secret police, yet Vienna remained Vienna.

When Beethoven arrived in late 1792, Vienna had not yet reached the peak it would achieve in the 1890s; its ancient walls were not torn down and replaced by the Ringstrasse until 1857, and the Danube on which it sat was a narrower stream than it is today (its branches were rerouted by dams late in the century). But it was already full of the airy Baroque buildings that continue to grace its streets, and its quarter-million inhabitants (Paris had half a million, London nearly a million) bustled throughout the city, drinking in cafés—and flocking to the concert halls.

For thirty-five years, they would flock to hear Beethoven; in 1827, thousands would flock to his funeral. If it was the rule in Vienna that "the fame of a man lasts only briefly," Beethoven would be the exception to that rule—as he was to so many others.

Emperor Joseph II.

Beethoven had various companions in Vienna, some of whom were attracted by his growing fame, others who genuinely cared for him. He spent part of each day in the cafés, talking about music, politics, and everything else under the sun (as well as consuming large quantities of wine).

But real intimacy he found easier at a distance. Beethoven maintained his closest friendships—with Stephan von Breuning, Franz Wegeler, the violinist Karl Amenda (1771–1836), and the cellist Nikolaus Zmeskall von Domanovecz (1759–1833)—chiefly by written correspondence. All too often, Beethoven's face-to-face encounters with his friends ended in terrible quarrels. Later, the composer would beg forgiveness—in a letter.

Similarly, Beethoven found it easy enough to fall in love—as long as the beloved was unattainable by virtue of being married, titled, or much younger than he was. Not long after his arrival in Vienna, he actually proposed to a singer from Bonn named Magdalena Willman, apparently out of the blue. Beethoven scarcely knew the young woman, and she turned him down—rather rudely, it is reported.

Beethoven couldn't even create a satisfactory home for himself. He moved frequently, occasionally residing in the home of a patron, occasionally with one of his brothers, but

Beethoven's friend and biographer, Franz Wegeler.

Beethoven strolling through a Viennese park.

most often alone; he had more than thirty different addresses during his thirty-five years in Vienna. Servants left his employ as frequently as he changed homes.

As soon as his finances permitted, Beethoven began leaving Vienna for the summer months, as did the nobility. He either visited summer residences or rented lodgings in country towns like Heiligenstadt. This was not the only way in which he imitated the upper crust of society; for most of his adult life, Beethoven encouraged his Viennese acquaintances to believe that the "van" in his name was merely a variant of the "von" that indicated noble birth.

By all accounts, the character traits that made him difficult (impossible, many would have said) were virtually innate, or at least formed early on by his lonely, troubled childhood. Yet for the entire second half of his life, Beethoven ascribed his behavior to the single torment that began sometime during this period. By 1802, it was clear that the worst thing that could happen to a musician was happening to him: there was something very wrong with his hearing—and it was getting worse.

Crisis After Crisis (1802–1812)

In the spring of 1802, Beethoven was in the grip of a severe depression. He had sustained a major disappointment when the director of the court theater turned down a proposal for a concert. But he was even more upset about his health and, especially, his ever-increasing deafness.

Beethoven's ear trumpet, an eighteenth-century hearing aid.

After consulting many doctors, Beethoven finally found one who told him—or at least *seemed* to say—what he wanted to hear: that resting his ears for a period of time might restore "the one sense that should be more perfect in [him] than in others." Upon learning of this potential remedy, Beethoven left Vienna for about six months. He went to the little town of Heiligenstadt, where he had previously spent several summers, in the desperate hope that solitude and quiet could accomplish what no other treatment had been able to do.

By this time, Beethoven was thirty-one years old. The next ten years would see an outpouring of music—the work of his "middle period"—that would by itself justify his place in musical history. It was a decade marked by intense emotional and spiritual anguish, as revealed in certain letters he wrote during this time, almost as if for the convenience of future biographers. He began and ended this crucial period with long, revealing letters that he never sent, but kept among his papers where they were found after his death. One of these was written at the end of his 1802 sojourn in the country and has become known as the "Heiligenstadt Testament." It is an extraordinary document, at once a letter, a mystery, a will, and a cry from the heart.

Written in two parts dated October 6 and 10, 1802, respectively, this document is, on its face, a letter to Caspar Carl and Nikolaus Johann. Mysteriously, however, Beethoven actually addressed the letter "To my brothers Carl and _____ Beethoven." He repeated the phrase—including the blank—not once, but twice within the body of the letter: "my brothers Carl and _____."

Nikolaus Johann van Beethoven, the brother whose name Beethoven could not bring himself to write down in his letter from Heiligenstadt.

The composer in the country: Beethoven at Heiligenstadt.

Biographers have wrestled with these blanks ever since, but unfortunately to no avail. Was Beethoven angry with Nikolaus Johann? Was he unable to write down the name that had also belonged to his father? No one has yet come up with a satisfactory resolution to this mystery.

The ostensible purpose of the letter was to convey Beethoven's wishes for the disposition of his property after his death. But the document was also clearly meant for posterity. In the circumlocutory language of the day—which paralleled his own muddled understanding of himself—Beethoven narrated the story of his deafness, climaxing with an account of his near-suicidal despair over its apparent intractability. Virtue, he wrote, was all that had kept him from killing himself.

Beethoven's cry from the heart, the "Heiligenstadt Testament."

The Heiligenstadt cure had failed, but perhaps the Heiligenstadt Testament had exorcised his despair. Not long after this outpouring of emotion, Beethoven returned to Vienna, where he resumed his life as he had left it six months earlier.

By Beethoven's own account, few were aware of his hearing loss. He had managed to conceal it, at the cost, he claimed, of appearing unsociable and rude. His deafness continued to elude discovery for most of the subsequent decade, during which the composer became ever more successful.

Beethoven was creating increasingly massive pieces. In fact, it was during this period that he composed much of his best-known work: the Violin Sonata in A Minor, Op. 47 (the "Kreutzer"); the Piano Sonatas No. 21 in C Major, Op. 53 (the "Waldstein"), and No. 23 in F Minor, Op. 57 (the "Appassionata"); the Razumovsky Quartets, Op. 59; the Violin Concerto in D Major, Op. 61; the Piano Concerto No. 5, Op. 73 (the "Emperor"); the first version of *Fidelio*; and the Second, Third, Fourth, Fifth, and Sixth Symphonies.

It was the Symphony No. 3 in E-flat, Op. 55, that inaugurated in 1804 what is known as the heroic period of Beethoven's work. He first dedicated the symphony to Napoleon, whom he had

The title page of Beethoven's Third Symphony, the "Eroica," with its original dedication to Napoleon crossed out and rewritten.

The revolutionary painter Jacques Louis David's portrait of Napoleon leading the French to glory.

admired as a great liberator; but while he was preparing the piece for publication, he heard that Napoleon had proclaimed himself emperor. Legend has it that Beethoven furiously crossed out the dedication, exclaiming, "So he, too, is nothing more than an ordinary

Napoleon Bonaparte (1769–1821)

The meteoric rise and fall of Napoleon Bonaparte touched every life in Europe and captured the imagination of generations to come.

Napoleon was born in Corsica to an Italian family in 1769. After an undistinguished military education, he was appointed a second lieutenant in the French army at age sixteen. The Revolution and the subsequent European war provided a scope for his military genius that the academy had not; he was a brigadier general at age twenty-four.

In 1795, Napoleon's decisiveness against counterrevolutionary insurgence in Paris saved the republic. A year later, he married Josephine de Beauharnais (1763–1814). In 1798, he undertook an aggressive campaign against England by invading Egypt. Although the campaign failed, Napoleon continued to rise. The coup d'état he led in November 1799 ended the seven-year-old republic; France became a military dictatorship with Napoleon at its head as "first consul." Elected "consul for life" in 1802, he proclaimed himself emperor two years later.

The sweeping reforms Napoleon instituted were genuine, effective, and in large measure, lasting. He modernized France's administrative and judicial systems, its finances, and its army; he created public secondary-school education; and he reiterated revolutionary principles of equality under the law.

But his territorial ambitions grew. After a short-lived peace in 1802, Napoleon's aggression provoked England to war one year later. England's triumph in 1805 over the combined French and Spanish navies at Cape Trafalgar off the coast of Spain forced Napoleon to seek new allies. His 1807 Treaty of Tilsit with Czar Alexander I (1777–1825) divided most of Europe between France and Russia; seeking to secure his power, Napoleon installed his own relatives as heads of state in the countries he had won, and he planned a Europe-wide blockade of England that would finally defeat his last enemy.

His dynastic dreams swelled despite an 1808–1809 insurrection in Spain. He and Josephine were childless (though she had children by her first husband). In 1810, he divorced her and married the Austrian Archduchess Marie Louise (1791–1847), daughter of Emperor Francis II.

But in 1812, Napoleon undertook what was to be a disastrous invasion against his former ally Russia, and the tide turned against him. Two years later, after defeat upon defeat, he was forced to abdicate. Exiled to the Mediterranean island of Elba, he continued to intrigue, invading France with an army of Napoleonic loyalists in 1815.

His restoration, which lasted one hundred days, was brought to an end by Waterloo. This time, the monarchs of Europe exiled the persistent warrior to the tiny island of St. Helena in the south Atlantic. Napoleon died there in 1821, probably of stomach cancer, his legacy the open question it remains today.

Napoleon as Emperor, by David.

Just as Beethoven's music was inspired in part by the political events of his time, so were the works of many of his artistic contemporaries, including Eugène Delacroix, pictured here in a self-portrait.

man!" Beethoven retitled the work the "Symphony Eroica" and wrote under the title, "to celebrate the memory of a great man." His vision of Napoleon remained ambivalent ever after.

All during this time, Beethoven's world was engulfed in war. Napoleon's soldiers were actually inside Vienna when Haydn died in 1809. Beethoven, along with the rest of Vienna, mourned the old master, though he ultimately claimed to have learned little or nothing from the late composer.

The war was causing rapid inflation, and all of Vienna was feeling the pinch. But when Beethoven started hinting that he might find it easier to live somewhere else, three patrons—Prince Joseph Lobkowitz, Prince Ferdinand Kinsky (1781–1812), and the emperor's brother, Archduke Rudolph of Austria (1788–1831)—

Late in her life, Bettina Brentano von Arnim made a number of unreliable assertions, one of which was that Beethoven had loved her.

granted the composer an annuity so generous that he would never have to worry about money again.

Meanwhile, Beethoven continued to have rather strained relations with his brothers. In the year 1806, Caspar Carl married his longtime lover, Johanna Reiss (c. 1784–1868). Four months later, their son Karl was born. Beethoven hated Johanna and the marriage, but came to care so deeply for his only nephew that he tried to adopt him after Caspar Carl died. Then, in 1812, Beethoven made a serious effort to separate Nikolaus Johann from the woman he loved, Therese Obermayer (1787–1828), an effort that the lovers thwarted by marrying each other. They remained substantially estranged from Beethoven for most of his remaining life.

Throughout this period, Beethoven himself was, as one biographer stated, never out of love—but never in love for very long. Apparently, though, no one was in love with him. The women he pursued were usually indifferent to his attentions. (In fact, there is considerable evidence that Beethoven, who was constantly being rejected by the women he courted, had a sex life that consisted almost entirely of relations with prostitutes.)

Among the unattainable women he wooed was the young Countess Giulietta Guicciardi (1784–1856), "a dear, charming girl," he wrote to a friend, "who loves me and whom I love." He dedicated the "Moonlight" Sonata to her in 1802—she was barely eighteen years old at the time, and he was thirty-two—but a year later she married Count Wenzel Robert von Gallenberg (1783–1839), a man of her own age and social class.

Then there was the widow Countess Josephine von Deym (1779–1821). Beethoven maintained his passion for her for a longer, albeit sporadic, period of time, though he did not appear to have marriage in mind. In any case, his three-year attempted seduction of the countess failed. Tactfully, she rejected him, claiming that she had taken vows of chastity upon her husband's death. Though there were men who could have told Beethoven otherwise, the composer chose to believe her (most of the time) and allowed their relationship to mellow into a platonic friendship.

In 1810, Beethoven made his second known marriage proposal, to the young Therese Malfatti (1792–1851), the daughter of an Italian doctor residing in Vienna. She, too, rejected Beethoven's hand.

But around the same time, Beethoven met and became friendly with several members of a family that would play a more significant role in his emotional life: the Brentano family. The writer Bettina Brentano (1785–1859) was a friend of Goethe; her brother Clemens (1778–1842) was a poet. In later years, Bettina claimed that she, too, had been among Beethoven's loves during that period, but the affair was almost certainly a figment of her imagination. It was probably her sister-in-law, Antonie ("Toni") Birkenstock Brentano (1780–1869), who inspired Beethoven's deepest passion.

The Woman He Loved

"My angel, my all, my very self…I will arrange it…that I can live with you….Much as you love me—I love you more….Is not our love truly a heavenly structure, and also as firm as the vaults of heaven?…I can live only wholly with you or not at all."

So read the contents of a letter found among Beethoven's papers after his death in 1827. Page after page, Beethoven poured out the hope that he and his beloved would overcome the unnamed obstacles standing between them.

Beethoven, as painted by Joseph Stieler in 1819.

Giulietta Guicciardi, to whom Beethoven dedicated the "Moonlight" Sonata. Early biographers mistakenly believed her to be the intended recipient of his "Immortal Beloved" letter as well.

But apparently he never sent the letter. Anton Schindler (1795–1864), who made off with many of Beethoven's effects after Ludwig's death—despite the fact that all the composer's possessions had been willed to Karl—published it in 1840, asserting that it had been written to Countess Giulietta Guicciardi in July 1806.

In fact, neither the name of its addressee nor the year in which it was written appeared anywhere in the letter. Beethoven had only dated it "Monday, July 6" and, later on, "July 7." Schindler himself added "1806" and simply assumed that the letter was intended for the countess.

By 1872, biographers—primarily the American Andrew Wheelock Thayer—had discovered Schindler's fraud, and for almost a century thereafter, scholars puzzled over two questions: When was the letter written? And, more important, to whom was

Countess Therese von Brunsvik was one of Beethoven's many passing loves.

it addressed? Who was the "immortal beloved" referred to in the most passionate love letter Beethoven ever wrote?

It was a genuine mystery. Certainly, Beethoven had cared, at least briefly, for many women, most of whom were out of his reach. Giulietta Guicciardi belonged on that long list, but so did the singer Magdalena Willman, Countess Josephine Deym, her sister Therese von Brunsvik, Therese Malfatti, and Antonie Brentano. Yet Beethoven's friends believed—and all other documentation suggests—that the composer never had a completely satisfying, reciprocated love affair.

Not until 1966 did a biographer come up with a solution that other scholars accepted; based on evidence within the letter, and on known facts about Beethoven's whereabouts and contacts during all the possible years during which the letter could have been written, Maynard Solomon argued persuasively that the letter had been intended for Antonie Brentano in July 1812.

If the intended recipient was indeed Antonie Brentano, Beethoven sustained another bitter disappointment shortly thereafter. Antonie and her husband, Franz, moved to Frankfurt later that year and never returned to Vienna.

In any case, the proposed solution to this mystifying puzzle only begs more questions. Why is there no other evidence of a relationship between Beethoven and Antonie Brentano? Were they actually lovers? Or did the relationship exist only in the mind of a tortured and desperately lonely man?

Everything but Joy (1812–1824)

Real or unreal, the debacle of the immortal beloved was Beethoven's last known search for romance. He was, if the theories as to the letter's date are correct, forty-one years old, and a new passion had taken root in his heart, a passion that would preoccupy him for the remaining fifteen years of his life.

It must have been quite clear to Beethoven by now that he was never going to enjoy a normal family life. His ever-advancing deafness continued to estrange him from the rest of the world. Loneliness had become his most constant companion. Fundamentally incapable of maintaining any kind of intimacy, he blamed everything and everyone for his failures except himself. Now, in a final instance of mad self-deception, Beethoven came to the astonishing conclusion that he, not his brother Caspar Carl—and certainly not Caspar Carl's detested wife, Johanna—was the true spiritual parent of his brother's son, Karl, the only member of the next generation of Beethovens.

But nothing stopped the flow of music, at least not for very long. In this, the final phase of his career, Beethoven was composing pieces unlike anything that had ever been written, and the audiences kept up with him. If anything, his popularity increased. Beethoven was not above ensuring this popularity with crowd-pleasers. In the years 1813 and 1814, he premiered his Seventh

The title page of Wellington's Victory.

The defeat of Napoleon and the ensuing Congress of Vienna sparked innumerable balls, galas, and public celebrations.

and Eighth Symphonies and a revised *Fidelio*; he also put out Wellington's Victory, Op. 91, his celebration of what appeared to be Napoleon's final defeat.

In 1814, the circus came to town—or rather, the Congress of Vienna. The most powerful men in Europe and their entire entourages filled Vienna, which glittered more brightly than ever as the work of remaking the map of Europe went on in back rooms. New audiences were exposed to Beethoven's works, embracing them as Vienna had.

Meanwhile, the ailing, deaf, and desperately unhappy composer did the one thing he could do well. He composed the "Hammerklavier" Sonata, Op. 106; Thirty-three Variations on a Waltz by Diabelli, Op. 120; and some less-known works, all the while creating what would be his symphonic masterpiece.

In 1815, Caspar Carl died, leaving Beethoven and Johanna as Karl's coguardians. Beethoven immediately undertook what turned out to be a decade-long battle against Johanna for possession of the then nine-year-old boy, whom he took to describing as his adopted son.

Franz Schubert (1797–1828)

n 1817, with Beethoven at the height of his career, a new bright star arose in the Viennese musical firmament: the young Franz Schubert.

By the age of twenty, Schubert had virtually invented the lied (German art song), having composed one of his masterpieces, "Gretchen at the Spinning Wheel," to words from Goethe's *Faust* when he was seventeen. Schubert would go on to master the symphony and many forms of chamber music before his tragically early death at thirty-one. Throughout his brief, meteoric career, he flirted with romanticism, but his lovely melodies were primarily expressed in the classical style of the masters who had preceded Beethoven.

The son of a schoolmaster, Schubert received his early musical education at home, then at the prestigious Stadtkonvict boarding school in Vienna, where he sang in the choir until he was fifteen. (While there, he was yet another of Antonio Salieri's famous pupils.)

At age seventeen, Schubert became a teacher, but he was unhappy in the role of musical instructor. For four years, he taught on and off; then in 1818 he quit teaching and devoted himself solely to music. He had already written hundreds of songs, five symphonies, a number of masses, chamber music (including the "Trout Quintet"), and six important piano sonatas. In 1817, he met Michael Vogl, the baritone who became his close friend and who popularized his songs in the best drawing rooms in Vienna. Yet commercial success eluded Schubert, and poverty haunted him for the rest of his career.

So did illness, beginning with what was probably syphilis in 1822. By 1824, however, performances of his music—at least of his songs—were increasing in frequency, and his new compositions became ever more complex and sophisticated. They followed one another with extraordinary rapidity: piano music, the song cycle *Die Schöne Müllerin* ("The Miller's Beautiful Daughter"), the String Quartet in A Major, and the "Death and the Maiden" Quartet.

He was well known in Vienna by then and traveling in the same circles as was Beethoven. But they had different admirers, Schubert having continued to work essentially in the classical tradition that Beethoven was leaving behind. There is no record of their having met until Beethoven lay dying in 1827, and even that encounter is uncertain.

Schubert did, however, walk in Beethoven's funeral procession. A year later, he gave his first and only public performance. He bought—at last—a piano with the profits, but did not have long to enjoy it. In October 1828, he contracted typhoid fever which brought about his death on the tenth of that month. There was no musician of any significant stature left in Vienna to attend his funeral.

Schubert in a Viennese salon.

Beethoven's nephew, Karl, upon whom the great composer lavished all the love that no one else had wanted.

The fight leaned one way, then another. Karl lived with his uncle, was sent to school, went back to his mother, was sent to school. Beethoven came close to winning, but suffered a stunning upset when the *Landsrecht*, or noble's court, in which he had sued for custody demanded documentary proof of his noble birth. When Beethoven was unable to produce such evidence—and thus forced to admit to all Vienna that he was in fact only a commoner—the suit was relegated to a lower court, where the process began all over again.

When he was in possession of the boy, Beethoven was—as anyone might have predicted—almost as inadequate a "parent" as Johann had been to him. Indeed, in one of the court proceedings, Karl testified that he feared maltreatment from his uncle. Their relationship remained turbulent until Beethoven was on his deathbed; the nephew, like so many others Beethoven had loved, broke his heart over and over again. It was never possible to give Beethoven what he thought he deserved.

By 1819, what was left of his hearing was fading rapidly. He was obliged to converse primarily in writing (incidentally providing posterity with the "conversation books" that would document so much of the last years of his life). Beethoven was still conducting performances of his work whenever possible; only after a disastrous dress rehearsal in 1822 did he finally concede that this practice was no longer possible.

It was about this time that the bane of Beethoven biographers, Anton Felix Schindler, entered the aging composer's life. A minor musician, Schindler not only worshiped the master obsequiously, but also managed to make himself very useful to his idol; Schindler virtually acted as an unpaid secretary for most of Beethoven's remaining years. (After Beethoven's death, he attempted to repay himself by absconding with—and seriously altering—a large number of Beethoven's papers.)

In the last years of his life, Beethoven desperately needed help. His health was deteriorating, and his eccentricities had deepened to the point that many thought him mad. Illness after illness, some more serious than others, kept him bedridden for weeks at a time. In 1821, he had a serious bout of what was diagnosed as rheumatic fever; jaundices, intestinal complaints, and respiratory ailments plagued him almost continually. Underlying it all, he may have had cirrhosis of the liver. Whatever the root of the problem, it was getting worse.

Yet in 1824, in the midst of all this suffering, came the crowning achievement of Beethoven's career. On May 7, at one of the most lavish concerts ever held in the always-lavish city of Vienna, Beethoven attended the premiere performance of his masterwork, the Symphony No. 9 in D Minor, Op. 125—the "Choral" Symphony, with its extraordinary setting of Schiller's "Ode to Joy"—and the *Missa Solemnis*.

The joy that the legendary composer had sought but never obtained had nevertheless inspired him to new heights, and the re-

The premiere of the Ninth Symphony.

sulting works were received with the admiration they deserved. It
is said that Beethoven, who had his back to the audience, could
neither hear nor see the adulation that was raining down on him.
When a friend urged him to turn around, the musical master was
moved almost to tears.

The event was, it turned out, a farewell of sorts. Beethoven
had more than mastered the symphony. Now he would leave behind the large orchestra he himself had created and turn his remaining efforts almost entirely to chamber music.

Beethoven, Goethe, and Schiller

Beethoven maintained a fifteen-year-long casual friendship with the towering literary giant of his time, Johann Wolfgang von Goethe (1749–1832). For years, he dreamed of setting to music Goethe's masterpiece, the mystical drama *Faust*. Although the inspired composer created songs from several of Goethe's poems and wrote the incidental music to Goethe's historical drama *Egmont*, *Faust* always eluded him.

In the end, it was the German writer Friedrich von Schiller (1759–1805) who inspired Beethoven's own masterpiece. Although Beethoven never actually met Schiller, the composer based the triumphant choral movement of his Ninth Symphony on Schiller's *An die Freude* ("Ode to Joy").

Goethe and Schiller, the two leading lights of German literature, were close friends, despite their very different lives. Goethe, who lived to be over eighty years old, never knew material need and achieved everything any man could want. The extent and range of his monumental attainments make him all but impossible to characterize. His early poems, novels, and dramas were significant contributions to the romantic German movement called *Sturm und Drang* ("storm and stress"); his first important novel, *Die Leiden des jungen Werthers* (*The Sorrows of Young Werther*), written when he was only twenty-five years old, brought him early fame.

Goethe was also a scientist who made important discoveries in biology and botany. (Indeed, Darwin was indebted to him.) A trip to Italy in his late thirties turned his focus toward classicism and led him to Christiane Vulpius, who would become the mother of his children and, eventually, his wife.

But most of the work that placed Goethe among the very greatest of European writers was written after he became friends with Schiller in 1788. Goethe was almost forty at

the time; Schiller, a dramatist and poet in the service of liberty, was under thirty. Schiller had suffered for liberty, having fled his native Württemberg to avoid imprisonment over his first play, *The Robbers*. He had lived in poverty, at least briefly, before writing the drama *Don Carlos* and the "Ode to Joy."

Schiller, as painted by Anton Graff.

Though he married happily shortly after he met Goethe, Schiller became ill within two years and lived the rest of his brief life under the shadow of chronic disease.

Schiller's best work, too, was written under Goethe's influence—or, rather, under the influence of their friendship. With Goethe's support, Schiller fought off illness long enough to write the historical dramas *Wallenstein*, *Maria Stuart*, and *Die Jungfrau von Orleans* ("The Maid of Orleans"), along with volumes of literary criticism.

When Schiller died at age forty-five, Goethe declared that he himself had lost "half of his existence." His words were a tribute to Schiller as well as to the friendship that had led German literature into the nineteenth century.

Finale (1825–1827)

At age fifty-four, Beethoven had two years left to live. The first would be productive; he spent it finishing his last six great string quartets—Op. 127, Op. 130–133, and Op. 135.

But Beethoven was neither happy nor well. His relationship with Karl was unsatisfactory, to say the least. The youth, then in his late teens, was living with Beethoven at the beginning of 1825, but he left in the spring to study at the Polytechnic Institute. The parting was extremely difficult for Beethoven, who shortly thereafter fell ill with a "serious abdominal complaint."

Even at a distance, Beethoven attempted to control every detail of his nephew's life. He convinced friends to spy on Karl, and sent letter after letter filled with demands and reproaches. Amazingly, Karl continued to write frequently, addressing his letters to "my dear father."

During the 1825 illness, Beethoven's doctor forbade him to drink alcohol, a prohibition Beethoven ignored almost from the start. Early in 1826, he fell ill again. The *sturm und drang* with Karl continued.

But in July 1825, something in Karl snapped. He bought a pistol, brought it home, and shot himself in the head, wounding himself seriously but not fatally.

Beethoven dropped everything to handle the crisis. Acting in accordance with his nephew's wishes, he arranged for Karl to enter the army as soon as he recovered. He even brought Karl to Nikolaus Johann's house in Gneixendorf to recuperate, though Beethoven and Nikolaus Johann had barely spoken for years. Ludwig and Karl spent the rest of the autumn there, each in need of recuperation; Beethoven's feet, legs, and stomach were swollen with edema.

By the time the two returned to Vienna in December, Beethoven was seriously ill with edema, called "dropsy" at the time, and jaundice; an operation was needed to relieve the swelling in his abdomen. Karl joined his regiment and wrote Beethoven often.

The surgery was only temporarily successful. Another operation was needed in January, followed by two more in February. It was clear to his friends—and indeed to all Vienna—that Beethoven was on his deathbed.

Tributes and good wishes poured in from all over Europe. The London Philharmonic Society voted him a £100 gift for "comforts" in his last moments. Some of the money was spent on wine, the last thing he needed, but by then it hardly mattered.

The monument erected in 1888 to mark Beethoven's grave in Vienna.

On March 23, Beethoven drafted a will leaving everything to Karl. The wine from the London Philharmonic arrived the next day. "Too late," Beethoven sighed. There is no record of his ever having spoken again. Two days later, the musical master lost consciousness. Beethoven died on March 26, 1827.

Thirty-six years earlier, Mozart had gone unnoticed to a pauper's grave. Beethoven received better treatment. A crowd of at least ten thousand Viennese followed his funeral to bid farewell to the "unlicked bear" who had composed the greatest music they had ever known.

Coda: A Composer and His Legacy

Beethoven left us his music, and we have cherished it ever since. But it is not only his music we have taken into our hearts; we have taken both his name and his face and created an image, an archetype, a myth.

It happened gradually. Throughout the nineteenth century, the romantic cult of Beethoven-worship grew. Biographers, among them his friends Franz Wegeler and Ferdinand Ries, as well as the hanger-on Anton Schindler, commenced plumbing Beethoven's life for its meanings almost before his body was cold. The romantic composers who followed him also helped create the legend; Richard Wagner (1813–1883), for one, described Beethoven's portrait as that of a "sublime...supernatural being."

By the late nineteenth century, any writer who wanted to conjure up romanticism or portray the power of music seized upon Beethoven as a subject. The Russian giant Leo Tolstoy (1828–1910) critiqued the destructiveness of undisciplined passion in his 1889 short story "The Kreutzer Sonata." France's Romain Rolland (1866–1944) wrote a short, adulatory biography at the turn of the century and then spent eight years on the ten-volume novel *Jean-Christophe*, which was inspired by the life of Beethoven.

In our own century, serious novelists and genre writers alike have continued to use Beethoven to set a mood or make a point. At the happy ending of E. C. Bentley's classic mystery *Trent's Last Case* (1913), the detective-hero asks his beloved to "play something on the piano that expresses...joy that has decided in favor of the universe." She responds with—what else?—"the theme in the last movement of the Ninth Symphony which is like the sound of the opening of the gates of Paradise." And in the climax of Aldous Huxley's mordant 1928 novel *Point Counterpoint*, the antihero Maurice Spandrell blows his brains out to the accompaniment of the String Quartet in A Minor, Op. 132.

But similar lists could be made for many composers; indeed, *Point Counterpoint* opens with the performance of a Bach flute concerto. What sets Beethoven apart is the depth and breadth to which his image has permeated the culture at large. His name, his face, the opening four notes of the Fifth Symphony are known to people who have never in their lives listened to what is now called classical music.

They have seen him in Charles Schultz' comic strip *Peanuts*, in which the child-pianist Schroeder has pounded away for thirty years at a toy piano bearing the bust of Beethoven. They have heard his name in Chuck Berry's rock and roll anthem "Roll Over, Beethoven." They have danced to the disco adaptation called "A Fifth of Beethoven."

Beethoven wanted to become a great composer, and he did. But he could never have imagined the extent to which his would become a household name.

Leo Tolstoy, author of the Russian classics Anna Karenina *and* War and Peace.

Suggested Reading

Beethoven's Life and Music

Anderson, Emily, ed. *The Letters of Beethoven*. New York: St. Martin's Press, 1961.

Cooper, Barry, ed. *The Beethoven Compendium*. London: Thames and Hudson, 1991.

Kennedy, Michael. *The Concise Oxford Dictionary of Music*, 3rd ed. Oxford/New York: Oxford University Press, 1988.

Kerman, Joseph, and Alan Tyson. *The New Grove Beethoven*. London/New York: W. W. Norton & Company, 1983.

Pauley, Reinhard G. *Music in the Classic Period*, 3rd ed. Englewood Cliffs, N.J.: Prentice Hall, 1988.

Rushton, Julian. *Classical Music: A Concise History from Gluck to Beethoven*. London: Thames and Hudson, 1986.

Solomon, Maynard. *Beethoven*. New York: Schirmer Books, 1977.

Wegeler, Franz, and Ferdinand Ries. *Beethoven Remembered*. Arlington, Va: Great Ocean Publishers, 1987 (orig. pub. in German 1838).

Europe and Austria in the Eighteenth and Nineteenth Centuries

Burns, Edward McNall; Philip Lee Ralph; Robert E. Leaner; and Standish Meacham. *World Civilizations*, 7th ed. New York/London: W. W. Norton Co., 1986.

Hofmann, Paul. *The Viennese: Splendor, Twilight and Exile*. New York: Anchor Press, 1988.

Wechsberg, Joseph. *Vienna, My Vienna*. New York: Macmillan, 1966.

Suggested Listening

Piano Music

Bagatelle in A Minor, WoO 59 ("Für Elise")
Sonata No. 8 in C Minor, Op. 13 ("Pathetique")
Sonata No. 21 in C, Op. 53 ("Waldstein")
Sonata No. 23 in F Minor, Op. 57 ("Appassionata")
Sonata No. 29 in B-flat, Op. 106 ("Hammerklavier")
Sonata No. 32 in C Minor, Op. 111
Thirty-three Variations on a Waltz by Diabelli, Op. 120

Chamber Music

Three Piano Trios, Op. 1
Six String Quartets, Op. 18
Violin and Piano Sonata in F Major, Op. 24 ("Spring")
Three String Quartets, Op. 59 ("Razumovsky")
Sonata in A (for piano and cello), Op. 69
String Quartet in E-flat, Op. 74 ("Harp")
String Quartet in F Minor, Op. 95
Trio in B-flat, Op. 97 ("Archduke")
String Quartet in E-flat, Op. 127
String Quartet in B-flat, Op. 130

String Quartet in C-sharp Minor, Op. 131
String Quartet in A Minor, Op. 132
Grosse Fugue in B-flat, Op. 133
String Quartet in F, Op. 135

Orchestral Music

Symphony No. 1 in C, Op. 21
Symphony No. 2 in D, Op. 36
Symphony No. 3 in E-flat, Op. 55 ("Eroica")
Triple Concerto in C (for piano, violin and cello), Op. 56
Piano Concerto No. 4 in G Major, Op. 58
Symphony No. 4 in B-flat, Op. 60
Violin Concerto in D, Op. 61
Coriolanus Overture, Op. 62
Symphony No. 5 in C Minor, Op. 67
Symphony No. 6 in F, Op. 68 ("Pastoral")
Piano Concerto No. 5 in E-flat, Op. 73 ("Emperor")
Egmont Overture and Incidental Music, Op. 84
Wellington's Victory, Op. 91
Symphony No. 7 in A, Op. 92
Symphony No. 8 in F, Op. 93
Symphony No. 9 in D Minor, Op. 125

Other

Fidelio, Op. 72 (opera)
Twelve Scottish Songs, Op. 108 (solo voice with piano trio)
Mass in D Major, Op. 123 ("Missa Solemnis")

Photography Credits

Index

A

Advertisements, *18*
Albrechtsberger, Johann Georg, 40, *40*
Alexander I (czar of Russia), 52
Amenda, Karl, 44
American Revolution, 12
Austria, 32

B

The Bastille, *8*
Beauharnais, Josephine de, 52
Beethoven, Anna Maria van, 19
Beethoven, Caspar Carl van, 17, 36, 42, 47, 48, 54, 59, 60
Beethoven, Franz Georg van, 20, 24
Beethoven, Johanna, 54, 59, 60, 62
Beethoven, Johann van, 11, 14, *14*, 15, 16, 17, 18, 19, 28, 33, 34
Beethoven, Karl, 54, 60, 62, *62*, 66, 67
Beethoven, Ludwig Maria van, 15
Beethoven, Ludwig van, *9, 34, 38, 45, 48, 50, 64*
  birth of, 12, 15
  childhood of, 16–21
  crisis in life of, 46–55
  death of, 66–67
  early composing career, 22–29
  final phase of career, 59–65
  finances of, 28, 31, 34, 36, 38, 45
  grave of, *67*
  health and hearing of, 36, 45, 46, 50, 60, 62, 63, 66
  homes of, *30, 37,* 44–45
  move to Vienna, 30–37
  music of, 25
  romantic life, 54–58
  social behavior of, 35–36, 44, 45
  success of, 38–45
Beethoven, Ludwig van (his grandfather), 11, *11,* 14, 15, 16, 17
Beethoven, Maria Magdalena Leym, 14–15, 17, 18, 19, 20, 21, 26, 33
Beethoven, Maria Margaretha van, 26
Beethoven, Nikolaus Johann van, 18, 42, 47, *47,* 48, 54, 66
Blake, William, 13
Bonn, Germany, 10, *10,* 11
Brentano family, 55
Brentano, Antonie "Toni" Birkenstock, 55, 58
Brentano, Clemens, 55
Brentano von Arnim, Bettina, *54,* 55
Breuning, Eleonore von, 24
Breuning, Stephan von, 24, *24,* 44
Brunsvik, Therese von, 58, *58*

Byron, Lord. *See* Gordon, George (Lord Byron).

C

Catherine the Great, 12
Charles VI (Holy Roman Emperor), 43
Coleridge, Samuel Taylor, 13
Communism, 12
Congress of Vienna (1814), 60

D

David, Jacques Louis, 13, *51, 52*
Delacroix, Eugène, *13*
Democracy, 12
Deym, Josephine von, 55, 58
Diabelli, Anton, 60
Diderot, Denis, 12
Domanovecz, Nikolaus Zmeskall von, 44
Dressler, Ernst Christoph, 21

E

Egypt, 52
Enlightenment, 11, 12, 26
Esterházy family, 32

F

France, 52
Francis of Lorraine, 43
Frederick the Great, 12
French Republic, 30
French Revolution, 12

G

Gallenberg, Wenzel Robert von, 55
Germany, 30
Goethe, Johann Wolfgang von, 13, 42, *42,* 55, 61, 65
Gordon, George (Lord Byron), 13
Goya, Francisco de, 13
Graff, Anton, *65*
Guicciardi, Giulietta, 55, 57, *57,* 58

H

Habsburg dynasty, 43
Haydn, Joseph, 20, 22, 25, 29, *29,* 30, 31, 34, 36, 40, 53
  music of, 32
Hegel, Georg Wilhelm Friedrich, 12, 13
Heiligenstadt Testament, 46–48, 49, *49*

Hess, Willy, 22
Holy Roman Empire 10, 43
Hume, David, 12

I
Industrial Revolution, 12

J
Joseph II (Holy Roman Emperor), 7, 12, 22, 28, 29, 43, *43*

K
Kant, Immanuel, 12, 42
Keats, John, 13
Keller, Maria Anna, 32
Kinsky, Ferdinand, 53
Kinsky, Georg, 22

L
Leopold II (Holy Roman Emperor), 28, *28*, 29, 43
Liberty Leading the People, 13
Lichnowsky, Christiane, 34, 35, *35*, 38
Lichnowsky, Karl, 34, 35, *35*, 38
Lobkowitz, Joseph, 38, *39*, 53
Louis XVI (king of France), 12

M
Malfatti, Therese, 55, 58
Maria Theresa, 12, 43
Marie Antoinette, 12
Marie Louise, 52
Marteleux, Joseph Engelbert, *23*
Marx, Karl, 13
Maximilian Franz, 22, 26
Maximilian Friedrich, 11, 22, *23*
Mozart, Wolfgang Amadeus, 17, 22, 25, 26, 27, *27*, 31, 32, 35, 36, 40, 67

N
Napoleon Bonaparte, 12, 13, 32, 50, 51, *51*, 52, *52*, 53, 60
Neefe, Christian Gottlob, 19, *19*, 21, 22, 23, 25, 26

O
Obermayer, Therese, 54

P
Pianos, *17*
Pols, Maria Josefa, 14, 17

R
Razumovsky, Count Andreas, 38
Reiss, Johanna. *See* Beethoven, Johanna.
Ries, Ferdinand, 20, *20*, 24
Ries, Franz, 20, 26
Romantic style, 35, 61
Rousseau, Jean-Jacques, 12
Rudolph (archduke of Austria), 53, *53*
Russia, 52

S
Salieri, Antonio, 40, *41*, 61
Schiller, Friedrich von, 13, 41, 65, *65*
Schindler, Anton Felix, 57, 63
Schubert, Franz, 61, *61*
Shelley, Percy Bysshe, 13
Simrock, Nikolaus, 20, *21*
Socialism, 12
Solomon, Maynard, 58
Spain, 52
Stieler, Joseph, *56*

T
Thayer, Andrew Wheelock, 57
Third Symphony ("Eroica"), *50*
Turner, Joseph, 13

V
Vienna, *33*, 43, *60*
Vogl, Michael, 61
Voltaire, François Marie Arouet de, 12

W
Waldstein, Ferdinand, 27, 31, *31*
War of the Austrian Succession, 43
Wegeler, Franz Gerhard, 24, 44, *44*
Wellington's Victory, *59*, 60
Willman, Magdalena, 44, 58
Wordsworth, William, 13